Warm Cups of Self-Care

Presented by Phillis Clements

Coffee & Conversation: Warm Cups of Self-Care

Cover by Angela Lofton-Moore of Info Princess

Inside photos from morguefile.com and pixabay.com

Published in the United States of America

Sunshine Solutions Publishing
9912 Business Park Drive, Ste. 170
Sacramento, CA 95827

Library of Congress Control Number 2019919307

ISBN-13: 9781670160522

Acknowledgements

This has been such a fantastic journey. I can barely find the words to express my gratitude, praise and awe at the wonderment of the women I had the pleasure of working with on this project. It really is a labor of love. I could not have accomplished such a phenomenal project without the contributions, dedication, friendship, and support of the amazing women in the Coffee & Conversation community.

I have to give special thanks to the contributing authors, Jacquelyn Smithson Howard, who has been in every compilation, Robin Robinson Myhand, Joy Normand, Jean Robinson, and Angela Lofton-Moore, who are returning contributors, Kenya Aissa, Linette Gill, Jean DiGiacomo, Pauline Haynes, Lauren Keeler, Michelle Keeler, Louise Umeki and Deanna Vestal who are first time contributors. They represent what the Coffee & Conversation community is all about.

I must also thank my awesome family, especially the man I love, who is always in my corner, lending an ear, eye and hand to help me achieve the goals I've set for myself personally and professionally. Not once have they questioned why I want to do what I do or tell me I couldn't do it.

THANK YOU for that!

Dedication

This book is dedicated to women all over the world. We want you to know that there are women out there just like you; beautiful, kind, valued, important, and loved.

Be a positive light to one another.

Bless each other with a knowing smile.

Foreword

Some of the most important lessons we learn in life do not happen in a classroom or in a structured way. Often, the most important opportunities to gather information about any of life's most challenging situations come in conversations with those who are willing to share the precious resources of their time, space and wisdom.

The premise of this book, Coffee and Conversations Compilation: Warm Cups of Self Care, is based on a simple, yet revolutionary concept: loving Your Self. As a trauma psychiatrist, I often ask people to list who they love. Sometimes the list is short and other times it is long. However, the thread that runs most commonly through that question is they often forget to list themselves. Worse yet, some intentionally leave Self off of the "love list."

We live in an era where we are constantly bombarded with messages that cause us to compare ourselves to others, implicitly and explicitly. We are told by people we love and trust, that we are "too much" of one thing, or "not enough" of the other. The words exchanged even by loved ones are too often damaging to our psyche and tend to program our beliefs about ourselves. Very rarely do we attend to the importance of learning to give and receive unconditional love, in our thoughts, words and actions, to ourselves and others.

In that context, what a gift this book can be to the reader! The words and thoughts in this book have been crafted with you in mind. Accepting you exactly as you are, with a message of Good Enough, delivered with warm regards and a prayer that you are able to absorb the loving message delivered through this text.

You are special, unique, remarkable, imperfectly perfect and deserving of the peace, joy and truth that can be found in emotionally safe conversations between Creators, determined to love their way into emotional, psychological and spiritual wellness.

Cheers,
Dr. Alauna
Trauma Psychiatrist

Table of Contents

"Self-care is how you take your power back."

~Lalah Delia

Preface

This book is a labor of love, adventure, inspiration and laughter. As women, we assume a myriad of roles; none of which are dedicated to our own self-care. As individuals, it is critical that we recognize the importance of our own comfort and happiness. It is NOT selfish to think about our own desires and dreams.

If we don't care for ourselves, we won't be around to take care of others. If you have taken a trip on an airplane, then you will recognize this. The flight attendant tells us during the safety presentation, "place the oxygen mask on your face first. If you don't save yourself, you won't be able to save anyone else." This is what the Coffee and Conversation membership community is all about – being a special tank of oxygen just for women.

Our Coffee and Conversation community is a wonderful group of intelligent, caring and gifted women who provide the much-needed environment of warmth, truth, love and support. We have been meeting once a month, for four years now, sharing stories, experiences, laughter and tears in a safe and positive environment.

Perhaps you will learn something new or confirm what you've known all along. In either case, it is our hope that the stories and expressions shared on the following pages will inspire you, make you laugh and uplift you.

"Our bodies are our gardens to which our wills are gardeners"

~William Shakespeare

Exercise

Jean Robinson

"One", I breathe in
"Two", I breathe out
Up, down
Huff, puff
The morning ritual continues

I look over and see them
Grinning at me with disdain
As I get up
They scurry away
Under and behind everything

But they always return with their families
They are prolific
Wantonly reproducing
Just like their namesakes
Dust bunnies

What is Self-Care, For Me?

Jacquelyn Smithson Howard

We've all been down the path of "I'm not enough" and may have decided to live there for a while. It's okay. Your true Self is trying to make your conscious Self re-align. Right now, you are out of sync with yourself. And the goal is to re-connect.

Spending some time each day, in a quiet space, will help you hear your inner Self. Put your fingers in your ears and speak gently to yourself. This will help you introduce yourself to the sound of your own voice.

Take some time to sit quietly with your eyes closed, perhaps using a mask over your eyes, to completely block out any light. Relax…and make sure every part of your body is comfortable. With your eyes closed and your body relaxed, your mind will start to show you all kinds of things…with your inner eyes, or your inside eyes, as I call them.

I love to dance and in oftentimes, I will get images of a supreme dancer twirling around with such grace and finesse. The images are abstract, but the movements are rhythmic and melodic. They dance across my eyes as if my inner being is being lifted on air to commune with the ebbs and flows in the vast reaches of the cosmos. It feels as if I am an infinite being in an infinite space.

The older I get, the better I feel. The better I feel, the easier it is to relate to others. I feel alive and engaged. I feel enriched with effortless ease, excited by every connection, electrically charged by the palpable positive energy of conscious beings strategically placed in every situation, for my good.

The older I get, the more I appreciate the older I get to be.

Life is sweet…and delicious. My body is soft and inviting to the touch, but strong enough to walk a mile in my stilettos. My mind is sharp enough to weigh my options, choose wisely, and make good decisions. My heart is strong enough to love unconditionally and allow myself to be loved in return.

My spirit is at peace, knowing that I am enough…for every encounter, in every moment that I am blessed to simply breathe. I know that with every breath there is a God-Wink designed only for me…a special connection between Source and me.

The gift is anticipating who or what will be chosen for my next God-Wink!

It's all about you! The importance of Self-Care

Robin Robinson-Myhand

I keep coming across articles and books about self-care without looking for them. I had no idea how overlooked and needed self-care is until this past year. I have a meetup group and this topic was the most attended.

Most of us take care of the outer stuff (hair, nails, makeup, clothes, shoes, purses). We've seen the outer stuff (grooming) being taken care of, so that comes easy to most of us. We have to look good, and this gives the impression of having it all together. Yet, we neglect the inner stuff (mind, body and spirit). In other words, we have been taught how to maintain and groom ourselves and have not been taught how to love ourselves. I asked myself why this is. Well, I think it's because most of us don't know how. If you don't see it and haven't been exposed to it, then how do you do it?

Most of us emulate what we have seen in our households with regard to self-care. As women, we oftentimes are doing for others and neglecting ourselves. Many of us have the role of wife, mother, daughter and this often puts us in caretaker mode. This oftentimes leaves us feeling underappreciated and overworked, and teaches others to take us for granted. This leads many of us to be seen as, and become control freaks and micromanagers. This often creates the inability to admit that we need help and the ability to accept and ask for help.

On top of caring for our families we are just too busy with work, social schedules, digital media, social media, and 250+ TV stations, to name a few. It seems like most of us are always ripping and running, and not for us. When do we have time for ourselves? Let's not forget about the inability to say "No". Many of us are over accommodating and over nurturing others at our expense.

For many women the idea of self-care is selfish, impractical, and just foreign. Well, it's not. We all need maintenance, yes maintenance. If you don't take care of your car what happens? It breaks down. The same thing will happen to us if we don't take care of ourselves. We will have a breakdown, be it emotional, physical or spiritual. It will impact our lives significantly.

As I am writing this chapter, I received an email from a mentor of mine. The headline, "Can I share something personal"? It caught my attention. She goes on to say that "over the last 60 days I've spent more time taking care of me, my body, and my health than the last two plus years altogether. Unfortunately, I waited way too long to take care of myself in this way." Basically, she is dealing with digestive, thyroid, adrenal, and orthopedic issues.

Remember, in the beginning I stated that I keep coming across articles about self-care. I view it as a reminder to me to make time for me.

"Caring for myself is not self-indulgent, it is self-preservation, and
That is an act of political warfare".

This is a sentence taken from the epilogue in Audre Lorde's book, A Burst of Light. Ms. Lorde was dealing with, not only breast cancer, but finding out that it had also spread to her liver when this statement was made. It is an account of how the struggle for survival is a life struggle and a political struggle.

What struck me was "and this is an act of political warfare". Putting aside the fact that Ms. Lorde was a feminist, what she is referring to is the act of self-care not only being an act of survival, but a rebellion against the socially established gender roles assigned to women to put the needs of others over their own. The expectation for women to be all things to all people affects our health.

This brings me back to my point of us not knowing how to do self-care. We have been indoctrinated by societal roles to put the needs of others over our own. Our mothers have done it, their mothers have done it, and so on. We repeat what we see. To do anything else is rebellion, hence self-care = rebellion to many of us. Being rebellious, for many of us, is not seen as feminine or ideal. Who wants to take that challenge on? Going against the grain doesn't feel good and, it brings about a lot of pain and guilt.

There are key areas of each of our lives, and there are general principles for self-care. They are as follows:

The six areas of self-care are:

- Physical
- Psychological

- Emotional
- Spiritual
- Relationships
- Work

The general principles are:

- Take care of your physical health
- Manage your stress and reduce it where possible
- Honor your emotional and spiritual needs
- Nurture your relationships
- Find balance in your personal and work life

The reality is, if we don't take care of ourselves, who will? When we tend to ourselves and our needs, we blossom just like tending to a garden.

So how do you do self-care? Well guess what, there is no one way or right way to do self-care. The possibilities are endless. It's all about listening to your body and paying attention. The key is paying attention.

One of the best things you can do for yourself is to do nothing. Just do nothing. Get quiet, sit in silence, and do nothing. When's the last time you did that? There seems to be the perception that you have to actively do something to do self-care, I don't agree. The act of just "chilling" in itself, can be self-care. If that doesn't feel right for you, don't do it; it's just that simple.

If yoga, running, journaling, gardening, and reading aren't your thing, then don't do it. It won't work for you and you will end up resenting it. There are endless suggestions and list of things you can do for self-care. My definition of self-care is doing whatever you want to do that makes you happy.

Ask yourself, what brings me joy, what am I passionate about? Think back when you were young, what did you like to do? What do you like doing now? Start from there. Self-care only works when you do what you want without resistance.

We have to unlearn what we have been taught. We have to learn how to say 'No" and not worry about offending anyone. It's not easy, it takes time and it takes practice and it is worth it. You're worth it.

One of my favorite teachings about self-care comes from motivational speaker and life coach, Lisa Nichols. She talks about serving from the overflow. Many of us are natural servers, and therefore, over serve. So, how do you know when you are over serving? When you dread helping or doing something, it becomes painful, and you have become resentful, then you are over serving. You have to continually pour into yourself (self-care) in order to not over serve. In other words, serve from the saucer underneath the cup and not from the cup. Serve from the overflow.

With the ongoing practice of self-care comes self-love and self-esteem. Self-care is your own personal rebellion. What a beautiful way to rebel.

The Sacred Art of Divine Fearlessness

Kenya Aissa

Self-care rituals are the antithesis of self-shaming thoughts and behaviors. The simple acts of washing our hair, moisturizing our skin, or taking a walk send a message to our brain that we are special. We are important enough for time. Time, the most precious and finite gift, is so carelessly squandered in modern Western society. We're not necessarily aware of the lack of reverence that we give to time, as we often mislabel "wasting time" as "unwinding". The truth is, sometimes our habit of "unwinding" is really "winding up" the stress receptors in our brains, and the cortisol in our body.

If we are glued to the television watching violence, people screaming at each other, or women constantly being judged, there is a deep impact on us as individuals, on our spirit, and on our culture as women. There is so much fear and shame tied to the vulnerability of surrender, that we often fail to see vulnerability as a sign of strength, surrender as a path to joy, and both as an act of radical self-care. If we let go (of fear, of the walls that we put up, of shame that we sometimes don't understand because the onset occurred at a time that was "preunderstanding", of sadness, of anger, of emotional exhaustion, of hopelessness, of worthlessness), then what? What will catch us if we let go?

We must trust the universe. Trust that we can surrender and still end up alive and unbroken. Fractured, but not destroyed. Trust that the universe, the divine spirit, our own spirit, will catch us. The landing might be really bumpy. It might be covered in glass and nails and snails and pain and disappointment, but we will land and we will stand. We will move forward and speak love over our healing souls.

Go to a mirror, look directly into your eyes, and say this affirmation:

> ****I will no longer allow fear, shame, and a false sense of worthlessness to imprison me. I am worthy of an empowered, impassioned life, and I won't let anything deter me from living my dreams. The universe has a profound vision for me, and I'm held and supported by its love as I walk my path.****

If we embody the sacred feminine, we band together as a force of spirit. And we've seen the abject terror that erupts in factions of our society that have always considered themselves the powerful majority, when women come together fearlessly and with great confidence and humor! That very terror is a message that we can't ignore. We don't intend for our sacred femininity to be a threat. In fact, we are too busy doing our own thing to waste precious, finite time on the insecurities of others. But in doing the work that needs to be done, whether it be in our communities or our homes, we can't distract ourselves from ourselves.

If our pattern is to focus all of our energy outside of ourselves in an effort to stay productive and to appear awesome to others, we must carve out time for coming back to ourselves. Fear, shame, and feeling worthless aren't paralyzing 100% of the time. People aren't always deer in headlights, because we're not wild animals. We care what others think of us, and the desire to be worthy and the fear of being unloved launches us into action. Selfless action, productive action, even dangerous action. But our tasks don't make us worthy. We just ARE. No matter what we've been through, what we've done, or what we have, our very feminine essence is a divine gift.

Encourage her, pamper her, celebrate her, see her.
For she is worthy.

"When the well's dry, we know the worth of water."

~Benjamin Franklin

The Seasons

Jean J. DiGiacomo

As Summer is nearing its end, and Fall is on the horizon, I have been giving the seasons some thought; both in terms of making plans and decorating my planners, and in terms of my life. I am a 60-year-old retired public school teacher. I am a sober widow, with a 21-year-old son, and a lovely significant other. This is absolutely, positively, and without a doubt, not where I thought I would be at this stage of my life journey. I don't know exactly where I thought I'd be, but I do know this isn't it. I surely didn't see myself as a widow, or as someone who would need to be in recovery. However, I also know absolutely, positively, and without a doubt, this is exactly where I am supposed to be.

According to the traditional interpretation of the seasons of our lives, I am now in the Winter of mine. Age wise, this is true. I am far closer to the end of my time on this earth than I am to the time of my start here. I have found, however, each of my life seasons have had their own seasons within them. No matter what age I've been, I have experienced joy and sorrow, happiness and sadness, contentment and restlessness, beginnings and endings, hope and despair, feelings of uselessness and usefulness, and more.

My age season does not define what I experience in my day to day living. Sure, I have more aches and pains than I used to. I have more wrinkles, and gravity is certainly doing its job. (Seriously, when did my boobs start being under my armpits?) I am more aware that I won't live forever than I have ever been, but I don't really give it much thought. I don't have a bucket list. That just seems so exhausting to me; trying to cram in certain things before my body leaves this earth. I continue to thrive. I continue to experience all human emotions. I continue to question and seek answers.

Fall has always been my favorite season of the year. This is the season of life that is associated with nearing the end. Not for me. The Fall season of my life looked just like every other season of my life, just different in its unique happenings. I neither feared nor looked forward to it. It simply happened, and I simply lived it.

As for the Fall season of the year, I do not associate it with nearing the end, either. I will do my best to embrace and enjoy the signatures of the season: cooler days and chilly evenings, that cozy feeling of lamps coming on in homes earlier in the day, sweaters, leggings and Uggs, crunching leaves, the smell of wood burning, and pumpkin spice candles (Ok, I have already started using mine and it is not even September yet.) I will also, however, do my best to embrace the things that come with every season, both of the year and our lives: the joy and sorrow, the happiness and sadness, the contentment and restlessness, the beginnings and the endings, the hope and despair, and the feelings of uselessness and usefulness that are likely to occur. I have found these things, my friends, are the things that make up life-no matter what season we are in, either literally or figuratively.

Although I truly do "Love Fall Most of All" there is something to be said for every season of the year, just as there is something to be said, and to live through, for every season of life. I have found no season of my life to be better, or worse, than another; nor any to be more, or less, rewarding. I have found none to be singular, as all my seasons have included the defining marks of every other season. I have discovered that things are exactly the way they are supposed to be.

Do you have a favorite season of the year?

Have you found the seasons of your life, thus far, to include all the things I have learned them to include?

Has your experience been similar, or different, from mine?

"You get in life what you have the courage to ask for."

~Oprah Winfrey

The Wisdom of Solitaire

Jean Robinson

Life is unpredictable. It would be different if we could see around corners and avoid all those little missteps that trip us up. But where's the fun in that? Is there any excitement and wonder...without those unexpected twists and turns? And how can you learn, if you don't make any mistakes?

In real life, unlike playing a game of Solitaire on the computer, there are no flashing lights when you make a mistake. You aren't automatically given the option to replay your hand or reshuffle the cards. You have to live with your choices and 'play the hand you were dealt', accepting what happened and continuing forward. And yes, sometimes that may mean being alone; but being alone does not mean being lonely. There are worse things than being alone; such as feeling alone, even when you're not.

So do the things you need to do, to take care of yourself – eat healthy, get enough rest, exercise in moderation, socialize with friends, join a book club, start a hobby, take classes on topics that interest you. (Maybe even dare to use a pen to solve that challenging crossword puzzle!) Find time to do things that simply bring you joy, while appreciating all that is positive in your life.

Taking care of yourself is not being selfish. It's caring enough about yourself to want the best for you, which allows you to share your best self with others.

"Self-care is a deliberate choice to gift yourself with people, places, things, events, and opportunities that recharge our personal battery and promote whole health—body, mind, and spirit."

~Laurie Buchanan, PhD

It's Not Too Late to Reroute

Joy Normand

"Vitality shows in not only the ability to persist but the ability to start over." —F. Scott Fitzgerald

A year ago, my husband and I were driving from Sacramento to Sonoma, CA to attend our niece's wedding. The closer we got to our destination, the more congested the traffic became. In fact, we were only going about 5 miles per hour. It was like a parking lot on the freeway. We found out that this was one of the locations where the California wildfires had been burning. However, on this day, the fires had stopped. I knew this because I checked online before we left our house. So, we were wondering what was causing the slow down. Was there a bad accident? I wasn't too worried at first because the planner in me had anticipated that we may have some traffic delays. After all, we were heading towards the Bay Area. Well, it turns out that the drivers in front of us had slowed down to observe the hills that had been badly burned in the fires just days before we arrived at the spot. But nevertheless, I had my working compass, paper maps and my GPS app ready to reroute if needed.

And sometimes in life that's just what we have to do, reroute. It doesn't matter who you are, where you've been or what you've been through, it's not too late!

We all have dreams, goals and aspirations, but maybe you are not where you think you should be at this time in your life. Maybe you've had some life altering setbacks, such as a divorce, dealing with a rebellious child, helping a sick or elderly family member, or maybe you lost a job, or you feel that you are stuck in a dead-end job. Life happens! Life happens to us all. I am certainly no stranger to facing setbacks and losses in my own life. I've been stuck a few times myself. We know that in this life, we are going to face some challenges. I certainly understand how setbacks and struggles can get in the way of your dreams. I know firsthand what it's like to stare at a roadblock in life and wonder, *"where do I go from here?"*

Just two years ago, I was struggling on my job as a project manager. The funny thing is, I was making good money, but I lacked purpose. I had no energy. Also, I wasn't operating in my God-given gift. I knew I wasn't walking in my purpose. I longed for more. But as Steve Harvey says, "You have to JUMP", but I couldn't. I had family responsibilities and financial obligations. I had so many excuses. What if I fail? What if I'm not successful? What if it's not the right time? I felt stuck with no way out.

As women, we are gifted in so many ways at so many things, but sometimes finding where we fit in and how to leverage our unique talents and skills can be a struggle. The biggest obstacle to achieving our purpose is the fear that we cannot do it. But God said we are fearfully and wonderfully made! (*Psalm 139:14*) Sis, we are beautiful, we are called, we are chosen, we are wanted, and we are enough! And God came to have a relationship with us, and He has a purpose and a destiny for our life! We all can achieve great things if we follow our dreams. Ephesians 3:20 tells us that God is able to do exceedingly, abundantly above and beyond all that we could ever dare to hope, ask or think.

I had to find myself again and identify my purpose in life. I never knew that by discovering my purpose would be an avenue for me to help others to discover theirs as well and succeed in life so that they can live out their dreams. I believe there is a desire deep down inside of you. You know that feeing, that desire that will not go away? I knew there was more that God had placed down inside of me, and there was more I could offer. But I knew nothing was going to change about my situation if all I did was sit and wish things were different. I had to **R.E.R.O.U.T.E.**!

Refocus and move forward. I had to accept my past, know my worth and not stay stuck. When you stay stuck in the past, you cannot move forward. There is a quote that says: *"When you believe in what you have to offer and decide what matters most, then you will discover your true purpose."* (—anonymous) The key word here is "believe". I had to believe that God would turn things around, but it all had to start with me. I had to make the changes and choose to go a different route and move on. I had to step outside of my comfort zone. A simple mind-set shift will help you keep moving forward instead of remaining stuck, stagnant and complacent.

Eat healthier foods and get proper rest. *"The greatest wealth is health."* (—anonymous) I started eating healthier foods, getting more sleep and drinking lots of water. After I changed my diet and started getting more rest, I noticed I was able to manage my stress which led to me making better lifestyle choices.

Remove the mask and take responsibility. Stop holding onto grudges. I had to own up to my mistakes. I had to forgive myself and let go of the things that was weighing me down; feelings of resentment and bitterness. Unforgiveness can prevent us from receiving the blessings of God. It's a decision to feel sorry for yourself over something that happened. You're the one who decides. Do what matters today. The choice is yours.

Overcome obstacles and be confident. Stop worrying so much. I had to let go and let God lead the way. A lot of times we step ahead of God and then we get lost. Confidence is the fruit of trusting God. When we trust Him, we may not have all the answers, but we are confident that He does.

Unite with other like-minded women. Don't isolate yourself. Studies show that socializing is good for your brain. In a study published by the American Journal of Public Health, researchers found older women with significant social networks were 26 percent less likely to develop dementia. Also, be a blessing to others. Maya Angelou said it best: "Be a rainbow in someone else's cloud." When you spread goodness through generosity, it can have a profound effect on a person's life.

Take time to feed your soul and water your dreams. Stay balanced. Don't overload your schedule. Unwind and relax. Take a walk outside. Read books that build your self-confidence. Make it a daily routine to mediate, exercise and daydream. Discover your strengths. You are at your best when you are focusing on what makes you feel good. Joy comes from within yourself. Are you appreciating the little things and making the most of every day? You will still have ups and downs but strengthening your emotional well-being will allow you to weather the storms and enjoy the sunshine even more.

Expect that good things will happen in your future. Stop being afraid of what can go wrong and focus on what can go right. Have a positive attitude. Did you know that it takes as much personal energy to be negative as it does to be positive? Having a positive attitude helps you respond to people in a positive way. Studies show that a positive outlook is linked to a longer lifespan, better health and improved wellbeing. When you think and feel positively, you are more likely to create positive outcomes. Always be learning and growing. Start where you are. Give your worries to God. With God, nothing is impossible. Through faith, any impossibility can become possible. God's got it and He's got you!

I am happy to announce that I made a U-TURN and chased my dream! I designed a workshop to help women turn their dreams into plans, get clarity on their purpose and help them get unstuck. This one-day workshop has evolved into multiple events filled with inspiration, empowerment, support, lots of laughter and women from all walks of life. I've never looked back and I love my life!

Believe me when I say this is not coming from a place of pride. It's about living a life driven by purpose. It's about thriving and not just surviving. I encourage you to look within yourself to see what desires God has placed inside of you. When you feel God nudging you to move forward boldly, you have to answer the call. The purpose and plan God has for you is bigger and better than what we could have for ourselves. Nothing changes in our lives until we make a decision to move in a different direction.

It's not too late—you can reroute and start again!

"Nourishing yourself in a way that makes you blossom in the direction you want to go is attainable, and you are worth the effort."

~Deborah Day

Surrendering into Self Care

Pauline Haynes

Great faith. Great doubt. Great joy. Great revelation. Self-care is an act of courage – being mindfully observant. Self-care is cultural, generational, and spiritual. More importantly it is very personal - an inner journey. It is more than a list of do's and don'ts. It is a connection to your Higher self. Your God Self.

Surrender is not about giving up. Surrender is acquiescing to the depth and power of who you are at your core. Surrender is knowing your connection with the Universe that gives meaning to your existence. Your ability to be awed by the joy and wonder of all that this life is.

If you've read the preamble, you might have a further interest in this deep dive into who you are. Yes, my sister. Self-care is very personal. It's about YOU!

Getting beyond the grief. The shame; the blame; the history and intimacy of anger opens a doorway to truth telling. Your truth. Your vulnerability can be your greatest strength. Treat yourself tenderly, as you would your most precious and prized possession. YOU are!

This is an invitation to be awed by your magnificence. To allow your femininity, your sensuality, your grace, your strength, your tenderness, your wild woman to shine unapologetically. In the words of the Lebanese writer, Kahlil Gibran (Spiritual Sayings of Kahlil Gibran) "There are mysteries within the soul which no hypothesis can uncover and no guess can reveal."

The unspoken can make us afraid. Are you willing to be seen? To be heard? To be vulnerable? To be raw? To be real? To uncover the truth of who you are? Most importantly, are you ready to be honest? Honest with yourself. If reading this touches your heart. You are ready to embark on a journey of self-care.

"The present was an egg laid by the past that had the future inside its shell." ~ Zora Neal Hurston (Author, Anthropologist, Folklorist, Activist 1891-1960)

I write as an elder, a crone, a 73-year-old African Jamaican woman. My journey to this time, this place, has been tempestuous at times. At other times the joy and pleasure has been immense. I imagine you have also had the highs and the lows. I venture to say that if you're alive, an adult, a woman, you've had challenges!

Self-care is the ability to ride the vicissitudes of life like the slow ecstasy of tantric sex!

Without the journey, those experiences, the ability for radical humility would be lost. I would not be who I am today without all those experiences. Those challenges. Those ecstasies. Those tears. That laughter.

Understanding the journey that has brought me to this place is what makes me unique. The shifts, challenges, transitions have weathered me like a storm, and in the words of our dearly departed sister, Dr. Maya Angelou "...But still, like dust still I rise!"

The joy that is ever present for me, is the thought of my two children, and my eight grandchildren. I am enormously blessed and in humble gratitude.

I believe part of my purpose is to be grateful. When I stand in gratitude. When I breathe in gratitude.

When I breathe out gratitude. When I share gratitude. When gratitude becomes my daily mantra. I know I am in the flow and taking care of me.

It is not always possible to attempt or even think about self-care, at this time when there is a constant barrage of the visible and invisible toll that racism, sexism, poverty, xenophobia, hurricanes, tornadoes, mass shootings, global warming, and the politicking that is swirling around our world, our society, our community, our homes. It takes a toll!

I know. I am right there with you.

This climate infiltrates our psyche, our mental and emotional frame of mind. Our psychological health, our familial interactions, and everything about our personhood! Our physical safety and well-being is at odds with our calm and serenity.

Some days are easier – yes. The days when there's laughter in our heart, love in our midst, the sun is shining, food in our belly, a place to call home, friends and family who care about us, a bank account that meets or surpasses our needs, our health is perfect. And we stay away from the news!

Ah, the bliss of contemplation!

The gratitude we feel and express opens us up to hope and optimism for the future. We can make plans. We can laugh, we can dance we can breathe into the meaning of who we are.

Without hope, we wither!

These topics nudge us beyond an intellectual discourse. It goes to the heart of who we are being today. Right here. Right now.

Perhaps part of self-care is asking, simply, "Who am I?"

Have you ever stopped to ask that question, not in a frivolous way, but in a way that forces you to be still? Perhaps during times of prayer, meditation or taking time to BE.

To contemplate. To discern. By asking that question, my hope is that it reveals to you that you are more than your job, your title, the initials before or after your name, the zip code in which you live, the car you drive, the latest designer attire – clothing, shoes, purses, glasses and on and on…

Getting the spa treatment, the mani/pedi, and the massage. Those are important as are the fresh flowers, the scented candles, the walks in nature, the dinners out. You are deserving of those niceties. They feed you – externally.

I don't have a 10-bullet point list of do's, I offer you the opportunity to take time out to consider what it means to you to care for and about you.

But sister Friend, hear this:

I am interested for you, in your daring to find out who you are - really!

Not the version of your parents, your spouse, your best friend, your siblings, your bosses. This is a solo quest to get you to the best version of you.

As you contemplate that question, I submit to you the following quote from Mihaly Csikszentmihalyi (pronounced 'Me-high Cheek-sent-me-high') from his book "Flow: The Psychology of Optimal Experience."

"How we feel about ourselves, the joy we get from living, ultimately depends directly on how the mind filters and interprets everyday experiences.

Whether we are happy depends on inner harmony, not on the controls we are able to exert over the great forces of the universe.

Certainly, we should keep on learning how to master the external environment, because our physical survival may depend on it. But such mastery is not going to add one jot to how good we as individuals feel, or reduce the chaos of the world as we experience it. To do that we must learn to achieve mastery over consciousness itself."

What a profound statement! Something more to contemplate…

The relationships we have, do they sustain and uplift us, or are they a drain? How do we make sense of those? Sometimes we have to remember that people are in our lives because we conjure them up. They are there for a
reason and a season. Maybe they are there as our mirror. They are our teachers, our mentors, our friends, our confidants or even simply to piss us off!

I submit to you that self-care is the willingness to grieve, to be in gratitude, to be generous, to be forgiving, to recognize and affirm that each and every moment is extraordinary. When we multiply those moments. We can bask in the unpretentious and simple things. The beauty of the flowers, the birds, the trees, the animals, laughter, music. It takes us to an enlightened place that reveals the real YOU!

Forgiveness gives us freedom. The ability to breathe. To pick up the pieces and continue on. To save our souls. If Immaculee Illibigazia, (Left to Tell: Discovering God Amidst the Rwandan Holocaust) who with seven other women were huddled silently in a bathroom for 91 days as she listened to the Hutu give graphic details about how they murdered her family. This woman faced the murderer years later and forgave him.
That, I believe is the ultimate self-care!!

I feel quite sure I would not have that courage, dignity, love, grace, humanity for that level of forgiveness…but who knows!?

Breathe in the aura of your uniqueness. In the entire world, there is not another exactly like you. You are a one of a kind gem.

"If now isn't a good time for the truth. I don't know when we'll get to it." ~ Nikki Giovanni (Poet, Writer, Educator, Activist)

Play in the garden of your imagination. Let this day be your reawakening. Love yourself. You are enough!

You are a miracle!

Starting the Day

Jean Robinson

I love walking early in the morning past silent houses

As the bright moonlight illuminates slimy designs

Left on the path by slithery creatures

And feathered tree alarms chirp their plans for the day

The air fresh, cool and crisp

How wonderful if I could only emerge

From my cocoon of blankets

Maybe tomorrow

ABC

The ABCs of Self-Care

Jacquelyn Smithson Howard

This has been a long, hard journey for me. I hope you will walk the path with me. This is the path to my freedom, in health. Imagine, for a moment, that you are out of balance mentally and physically, while living your normal life. Now, imagine that your internal systems start to reveal an imbalance in silent ways...unobtrusive ways!

You don't feel anything changing from moment to moment because "life" is continuing to happen. You are going about your normal day doing the same normal things that you have done forever. So, let's move along and see what happens when the internal imbalances begin to stir.

I must alert you, first! This is a gentle warning that this entire episode is *"me"* talking to *"me"* about *"me."*

I'm going to start with the ***authentic accountability*** of self-care. It lives in the subconscious part of you. You know the right things to do, and you know the wrong things that you are doing daily, when it comes to your health. You just make excuses or set deadlines that you yourself don't even follow. You ignore these small warning signs.

This certainly leads you into the ***busyness burrows***, where you shelter into your excuse mode and create a story to justify your inaction. You immediately begin to compose ***creative causes*** to justify why it is perfectly fine for you stay in "nothing wrong here" mode. You are constantly convincing yourself that you are perfectly fine just as you are.

But, everything is not fine. Your clothes are getting larger, tighter, more expensive, and duller in colors and prints. You don't sleep as soundly as you should. Small aches and pains come and go so randomly that you are quick to dismiss them. Now, it is time for some ***direct discipline***. This is your first attempt to introduce your ***energetic ego*** to your ***favorite friend***...you...in order to establish a ***good grasp*** on some new concepts for ***healthier habits***!

You'll most likely be unaware of the ***intentional irony*** of this situation. This is because there are two parts of you. There is your subconscious side (EGO Self) and the conscious side (your TRUE Self). Your EGO wants everything to stay the same. Your TRUE Self wants you to live in your passion. So, the irony is that both sides of you are trying to help you be happy.

However, I'm going to need you to take a huge ***jump in judgment*** and give your EGO Self permission to go play elsewhere just for a few minutes, so we can ***kindle kinetics*** in a new ***lyrical language*** of a ***minced mindset*** so that we can set a ***new narrative.***

We are going to have to move quickly to ***override operations*** and ***pause preconditioned polar positions*** just long enough to ***quietly quell*** the ***rowdy revolt*** that is about to ensue. The EGO Self has a monkey-mind-motive that doesn't play well with others for long periods of time. So we have to move quickly to ***systematically saturate*** the monkey brain with enough cognitive neurology to transmit tactically new ideas and concepts that will ***technically transform*** your current "Whole Self" into a new state of what I call Y.U.M…which is an acronym I developed several years ago which means "Yes to U and Me."

Remember, this is still *"me"* talking to *"me"* about *"me."*

This is going to demand that you make an ***uncompromising ultimatum*** in order to maintain a ***veracious vibration*** and a ***wealth of wisdom*** to better control the ***xerotic xanthomas*** of the aging skin and body. Keep in mind that nothing will squelch your negative ***yatter in a yoctosecond***. You're going to have to stick with this for a while. There's an old wives tale that says everything good in life lasts "a moment on the lips and a lifetime on the hips." All of whatever is going on inside of you, outside of you, around you, and through you took a little longer than you are willing to admit. So, give yourself permission, in love and in peace, to create your own personal ***Zen zones***.

It is my hope that you will find your own Zen in your mind, body, and spirit…in your home and furnishings…in your fragrances, foods, sights and soothing sounds. I challenge you to start a new period of Y.U.M. Give yourself permission to all of the positive energy and vibrations of the Universe by saying "yes" to every opportunity that comes to you over the next year. Take a deep breath, go within, and rediscover your TRUE Self.

"Love yourself first, and everything else falls in line."

~Lucille Ball

I Turned 35 in Bali

Lauren Keeler

As a child, I was surrounded by strong women who I watched and learned from. My mother, who raised me on her own, wore an invisible cape. I'm convinced that she never slept. I don't know how she worked full time (as a nurse), went to school full time, volunteered at my school, had me in extracurricular activities, and managed to also be there for those she cared about. As a child I didn't realize the amount of energy and time she sacrificed.

I only have one job, no kids, and I'm tired every day! I don't know how she did everything but what I'm clear on now is that she did not engage in self-care. My grandmother was someone who I also watched and admired, she was a wife and mother of four, worked and volunteered at church and never engaged in self-care. Sure, there were the occasional hair and nail appointments, but from what I know about self-care, that wasn't much. After reflecting on my life, most of the women around me put others before themselves while saying that they were "okay." I know that wasn't the truth because I saw how exhausted and empty they were after pouring love and light into everyone but themselves. They were strong, supportive, and loving; yet I too, selfishly indulged in all they had to give.

Reflecting on my own journey through life and womanhood, the "strong" women who raised me didn't engage in self-care. Instead, they just prayed and persevered through life's challenges. That's how they were taught and what they showed me. If you asked them, "How do you respond to life's ups and downs?" Faith is the answer. I'm grateful for that lesson because my faith has truly brought me a mighty long way! Just the other day, I put on my gospel music as I rode to work and prayed, cried and shouted... that is still one of my "go to" coping skills. However, I have had to learn many other ways to feed my heart and soul. The one thing about life is that it keeps happening, whether you're ready for it or not. We experience joy and pain regularly and have learned to somehow survive. I became tired of being in survivor mode. Although I am grateful for every day that I wake up, I was tired of being tired. Tired of existing in a routine of being exhausted, frustrated, and on some levels, broken.

I've had my share of hardships throughout life: health issues, death of close loved ones, unemployment, miserable jobs, debt, injuries, disability, house fire, bad relationships... all of which I overcame, but stuck with me. I felt as if I had invisible scars and I knew there had to be a way to heal. I started with my foundation of faith for self-restoration. I felt some peace, but it wasn't enough. Even going to church did not provide me with a feeling of balance. I asked God to help me find my way.

My best friend introduced me to a mindfulness group. To be honest, I was judgmental of all the, what I saw as, "hippy dippy" stuff. Hugs from strangers, connecting with people on a deeper level, being aware of my own victim habits… this was something new and definitely challenging, but I kept going back. Through workshops, support of that group, and self-reflection, I was able to uncover a lot of the things I buried deep inside. My negative thoughts about myself and some of the choices I made throughout life had all been an antithesis to self- care or self-love. With that realization, I really began to see my responsibility to myself to at least try to be better. Although I have gained clarity, that doesn't mean I still haven't had my struggles.

I have a very demanding job. I work with adults and children who require me to support them with challenges that I can't even begin to describe. My job can be mentally, physically, and emotionally draining. I have found myself pouring most of my energy into work and feeling depleted. I have lots of people in my personal life who I love and have poured into them. Even though they show me reciprocity, I realized that I didn't pour enough love into myself. Just last year, I felt like a complete disaster. I was crying every day, sleeping every chance I got, having anxiety attacks, carrying negative thoughts, and felt hopeless. I isolated myself because I didn't think that version of me would be embraced. I was wrong. I lost faith in myself and those around me. I just felt like I was failing at life and couldn't find the strength to move forward.

So, I revisited my mindfulness group and participated in a workshop about love, intimacy and healing. Not romantic love, but self-love. And let me tell you how I woke the hell up there! I felt truly vulnerable and open after that weekend. I forgave myself for the "mistakes" I made and clearly saw the beauty in who I was and still becoming. I decided after the workshop that I was going to fall in love with myself and do what serves me. With that declaration, I made the choice not to participate in relationships and "situationships" which do not uplift me or help me grow. I reconnected with my creative side through painting, drawing, and writing. I have changed my eating habits. I watch how I talk to myself and stay mindful not to hold on to my negative thoughts. I have started to do things and go places which are new and sometimes scary to me. I have made a promise to see more of the world. I have chosen to strike out on my own with my career. I am growing in my spirituality and working to maintain balance between work and home. Most importantly, I am allowing myself to be vulnerable which has led me to fall in love with myself and find love with someone new. I am truly enjoying this journey.

As a token of love and self-care, I decided to honor my dreams and goals of world travel. Most recently I took a trip that only confirmed that the universe got me. I turned 35 in Bali! "What?! Is this real life?" I asked myself as I danced along the tide during the most beautiful sunset I could remember. I reflected on how blessed I was… where I had been even six months ago was a far cry from where I was in that moment. I felt like a child in that moment, in awe of the world around me and eager to learn and venture out. I experienced true bliss and to be honest, I had to take a step back and praise myself for giving me the best birthday gift. I was proud of me. I am proud of me and my growth. I'm proud of this journey of self-love that I'm on.

As I said before, life is a series of ups and downs. Rather than count myself out every time I fall, I've learned to stand on my new foundation of faith AND self-love. Whether I call it self-care or self-love, I have learned to honor myself through every part of my journey. I will continue to surround myself with positive people, take space when I need it, walk away from things which do not serve me, go to therapy, make healthy lifestyle choices, crush goals and do things that speak to my heart and soul.

We should all pour love and light into ourselves. To whomever reads this: Love, honor, and cherish ALL of yourself, pour light and love into the universe, and you will see what life truly can gift you with.

"Happiness is when what you think, what you say and what you do are in harmony."

~Mahatma Gandhi

Power of Purpose

Linette Gill

You can't make the sun not rise and set

You can't make the moon and stars stop
illuminating at night

You can't make time slow down or pause.

You can't make the law of attraction and
reciprocity not exist.

You can't make gravity quit.

All functioning like an orchestra
with powerful purpose
for every life cycle
above, on land and beneath

Flowers will bloom in the Spring

And then Summer with relentless heat

In the Fall leaves will turn colors
and blanket the ground
as Winter is ushered in with rain and snow

All functioning like an orchestra
with powerful purpose
for every life cycle
above, on land and beneath

All that is, will be
and will remain

Unless the Creator says,
STOP.

How can I, be a part
of this extraordinary power of purpose
that is unmatched and endless
with unmeasured strength?

How can I, find a rhythm?
in this purpose filled universe
that has continuous fusion of creativity
that is beyond my capability to comprehend

How can I maximize my existence?

How can I tap into this absolute consistency?

How can I become limitless in a unique purpose
providing a specific necessary part
of life's orchestra

that is?

All that is,

All that will be,

And All that which will remain

Until…
the creator says
STOP!

Self-Discovery | Self-Love | Self-Care | Self-Discipline

Angela Lofton-Moore

Self-Discovery -

This is a special year for me. 2019 is the year I turned 62! I still can't believe it myself, even though I have sort of been looking forward to that day. Physically and mentally, I still feel like I'm 35 and I truly consider that a very good thing.

When I entered my 50's, I promised myself that I would turn 60 without facial lines and wrinkles. Done! I promised myself that I would stay in top health. Done! I promised myself that I would be retired and taking it easy by the time I turned 62. OK, so here's where the problem comes in. You see, at age 60, when others my age wind down their careers and begin their highly anticipated decent into an easy, laid back, well-deserved retirement pace, I signed a 5-year lease on a building for a brand-new business. At that moment I became what is called a Hybrid Professional – a newly defined multi-faceted and multi-talented individual who cannot simply be described by one single word. I am an entrepreneur, a graphic designer, a business coach, trainer and educator. I was very proud of my new role - Hybrid Professional - but what in the world was I thinking?

Not only did I take on the task of starting my coworking space, WorkFlow Lounge, I also still run a now 10-year-old graphic design agency, along with our hobbies business, MoorePark Enterprises which, among other things, creates annual small batches of great tasting peach and plum wines through its MoorePark Orchards division. If that weren't enough, in the last 2 years, I also started a process server business, partnered in a Work Force Development business and created a nonprofit organization called Beyond The Village that provides small business development services, technology training, day programs for developmentally challenged adults and a community youth mentoring program. Needless to say, I am exhausted … A Lot!!

Self-Love -
At home, I am a wife of 27 years to my wonderful husband, Sidney. I am also stepmom to 4 loving adults whom I adore with all my heart. They have blessed us with wonderful grand kids and the smartest and most adorable great grand kids. In addition, for 3 years before we opened our newest

business in 2017, we also took on the full-time responsibility of caring for my mother, Rosie, who was diagnosed with dementia. Last but not least, at that time we had 3 fur babies – Mocha, Snipper and Luke - that wanted and deserved my attention. Bottom line, my life is filled with love, joy and a lot of happiness. Yet and still, I needed to manage myself into a work/home balance that allows me to be authentic in my personal life, energetic in my work life and do it all while making it look super easy.

Taking on this much at this stage in my life comes with many challenges, not the least of which is the stress of growing several brand-new businesses, running existing businesses, taking care of Rosie, and all that comes along with that. I know that if I am going to survive the next 3 years (I have a 5-year business exit strategy), I will need to take care of myself.

I decided to immerse myself into figuring out the best way to retain my sanity while doing everything that needs to be done on a daily basis. I am very fortunate to have the support of close friends, family and associates who have my best interest at heart. That alone goes a long way toward making me more effective in my quest to achieve my life goals. A great support system and great network of truly supportive people are a big part of my self-care program.

Self-Care -
About 18 months ago, 6 months into my new coworking space venture, through the use of some guided meditation, I became more acutely aware of my ability to engage the Universe to create the kind of life, business and personal, I wanted to create for myself. I decided to take a deeper dive into the science of quantum physics to learn more about the phenomenon of the Law of Attraction. While the words "Law of Attraction" may be familiar to many people, few actually understand the significance or exactly how to engage the Universe to create the life they would like to have. While I've only recently engaged the Universe on purpose to help me create the life I now enjoy, my husband informed me that I've been doing this for as long as he's known me, pointing out that the Lexus I manifested in 1994 was the result of a picture of said Lexus I mounted on my bathroom mirror. He also reminded me that I came up with the name Mocha about 6 months before we found and adopted our Chocolate Lab in 2005, that I've gotten every job that I've ever put my mind to getting and that the home we bought in 2006 is an

exact representation of the "dream home" I described to him a few years earlier.

With that said, my daily routine is a large part of my new diverse and alternative lifestyle of balancing my work life and my personal life into something manageable. It goes something like this …

I get up every morning between 5:00 – 5:30 am. First thing I do is drink at least 8 oz of room temperature water which helps my internal organs flush out impurities. I grab my phone and glasses and head downstairs, sometimes in the company of my fur baby Luke who loves to avail himself of our morning alone time to get some one-on-one snuggles in with me. I lay on my leather sofa and rest my legs on a stack of pillows to keep them above my heart level. I find a favorite guided morning meditation on my phone, close my eyes and, while focusing on my breathing, take in the words and imagery of what I hear. Most meditations I engage with are 10-15 minutes in length which is a perfect time for me to bring my thoughts into positive territory and eliminate the negative thoughts that might try to sneak in on me first thing in the morning. I do acknowledge anything negative that is going on, but then let it go. Negativity has no place in my life these days and anything, or anyone, who brings it to me will find themselves removed from my personal space immediately.

Once my meditation is done, I spend about 10 – 15 minutes catching up on my favorite game, Words With Friends. I have a large community of players and I enjoy engaging my brain in the activity of creating words from a pile of scrabble-style letters. It's my way to get my brain active early in the day. Then, it's on to coffee! One of my rituals is to grind whole coffee beans into an aromatic brown powder to make the coffee Sidney and I love. To us there is nothing quite like freshly ground coffee beans turned into deliciously brewed coffee. While I'm enjoying my first cup of my favorite morning liquid, I cruise through my many social media channels and create words of love, inspiration and gratitude to hopefully bring a smile to the faces of those who follow and support me.

Next on my morning agenda is the care and feeding of my fur baby Luke and my feathered friends. Our backyard is home to a huge variety of birds including doves, quail, blue birds, robins and many yet unidentified species of birds that visit every morning and have breakfast right outside of my family room window. We have also found that a cottontail rabbit has made MoorePark his home which fascinates Luke to no end.

I usually keep my phone in my robe so that I can enjoy calming meditation music while going through my morning routine. All of this helps me to set the tone for my days which sometimes tend to be 12 or more hours long.

Two other very important parts of my work/home balance strategy are the level of nutrition and rest I plan for myself. I have no problems getting 6-8 hours of sleep each night. I'm fortunate that way. I rarely ever have insomnia or experience sleeplessness. I am also the princess of the power nap. I can make myself go to sleep at any given moment (which drives my husband crazy), decide how long I want to sleep and wake up within 5-10 of my desired sleep time, fully rested. I attribute that to my insistence to not take pharmaceutical medications unless it is absolutely, without a doubt necessary.

Earlier this year, I dedicated one month to eating no bread, no pasta and no processed sugar. The results of that 30-day experiment were eye opening for me. In recent years, I have been suffering from slight hip joint and lower back pains that have no muscular skeletal causes to point to. As I mentioned, I dislike taking pharmaceuticals to relieve pain and will take only aspirin to alleviate my pain.

Within 3 days of starting my no sugar/bread/pasta regimen, all of my joint pain disappeared. I experienced no pain for the entire rest of the month of July, which was like heaven. By eliminating those three elements from my diet, I was able to also lose 10.2lbs in those 30 days, another great bonus of the program. This was the second time I have done this same 30-day plan. The first one back in 2016 allowed me to lose 22lbs, mainly because I was still eating a lot of sugar back then, especially in my coffee creamer. I never returned to my full-sugar coffee creamer and have walked away from many of the high sugar items I used to love to indulge in.

I love to cook and our meals, while containing a lot of the things we love, are centered around a lot of fruits and fresh vegetables. The more colorful our meals are, the better we like them. We both love salads and aren't bothered by the occasional meatless meals. We do not shy away from beef, pork, bacon or any of the other meats we love, we simply eat less of them and prepare them in a way that is healthier for us. Neither my husband, who is almost 78, nor I suffer from any of the normal aging diseases and we attribute that to our lifestyle of eating right, loving and laughing daily and staying away from those things that we know cause us discomfort. Since my July no sugar/pasta/bread program, I have added those items back into my diet very cautiously listening to my body every step of the way. About a month ago, I ordered lunch into the office. After eating 2 cookies for "breakfast", I ordered Spaghetti Factory pasta which came with one of their wonderful loaves of warm bread. I ate my pasta and some of the bread. 2 days later I was in excruciating pain from my lower back down my left leg to my knee. Of course, I immediately knew what had caused that and I went back to eliminating pasta, most bread and most sugar from my diet, giving me the relief I knew I'd get. My advice is to listen to your body and don't blindly take medication to mask problems that you can fix yourself. I honestly believe that because I never bought into the "take this pill for this and that pill for that" scenario, I am now able to avoid the trap of taking medications that will require me to take additional medications to fix the side effects of the first medications.

Self-Discipline -
You may have noticed two things ... I do not turn on the television or read email first thing in the morning. At the MoorePark house, we stopped turning on the television early in the morning about 15 years ago because there is far too much negativity in the news, and we decided to avoid bringing that negativity into our personal space as part of our morning routine. While emails are not necessarily negative in nature, they do immediately take you into work mode in a way that you sometimes can't retreat from for several hours. I set my work hours and make myself available to clients from 9:00am to 6:00pm, Monday through Friday, and I strictly adhere to that schedule about 95% of the time. As a business owner there will always be an exception to every rule, but I try to make sure that those exceptions are kept to a minimum.

In order to maintain my work / home life balance there are several rules that I've established that are absolutely non-negotiable. My life is hectic, by choice – MY CHOICE. Nevertheless, people seem to find it necessary to attempt to inject themselves into my life at their leisure. This is something I no longer allow. The following rules have helped me …

1. "NO" is a complete sentence!
2. I don't allow other people's emergencies to become mine
3. When life becomes stressful, I close my eyes and count my blessings
4. Poor planning on someone else's part, does not constitute an emergency for me
5. When people show me who they are, I believe them the first time
6. Success to me is doing my best at all times
7. If you want more than 5 minutes of my time, schedule it in advance
8. Once you lose my trust, it will be very hard to get it back
9. What you think of me is none of my business
10. If you disagree with how I run my life, feel free to remove yourself

While this is nowhere near a complete list of the rules that help me manage my life these days, it is a good representation. I thrive on being busy, creating beauty, helping people succeed, spreading love and positivity, and living my life the best way possible. I plan to live to age 120.

That may sound crazy to people but it's my goal. As long as my body, mind and spirit are willing and able, I'm all in!

"Dream Big and Trust The Universe"

"Sometimes the most important thing in a whole day is the rest we take between two deep breaths."

~Etty Hillesum

Morning Walk

Jean Robinson

Cool crisp air is filled with convivial choral chirping

Wind-blown twigs create designs on walkways

Orange kumquats decorate like ornaments

Wintered trees filigreed against a slate sky

Golden carpet stretches across lawns

All is quiet waiting for the rain

Fierce

Check Yourself

Phillis Clements

Belief is a powerful thing.

What we believe and what we value directly impacts the choices we make and the actions we take. At some point we must take responsibility for what we contribute to the experiences and situations we encounter. While there are definite influences and circumstances we cannot completely control, we can definitely control how we respond to them.

I have a super power for this. It's called CHOICE.

I use it every day and in every way possible. YOU can too! CHOICE is your super power. No one can take it from you – EVER!

Just picture the long flowing cape behind you billowing in the breeze with a gigantic "C" in between your shoulder blades. When it gets cold you can use that cape to wrap yourself up for warmth and when it's too hot it makes for a great blanket to sit on at the beach watching the waves move in and out or for a simple picnic in the park.

You get to choose in every situation how you respond to it. Does this mean every choice will be easy? No, it doesn't. Choices are options. Some choices will be completely crappy. You choose which consequence of the choices you can live with and move forward from there. Once you choose, you decide how you will proceed. Taking action is the next step.

This is the same process you use when determining how you will take care of you. Making self-care a priority for you is a CHOICE.

You also get to choose what self-care looks like for you. Give it some thought. Take the time to really think about what you need. Ask yourself some questions to help you gain clarity.

1) What do I need to feel cared for? (not from others, from you)
2) What would feeling rested look like for me? (a 10-minute meditation or a 15-minute nap)
3) When was the last time I did something I really enjoyed, just for the fun of it? (not work related)
4) What would it feel like to relax? (a spa day or a bubble bath)

You can probably think of a few more questions to ask yourself. Be honest with yourself. You don't have to tell anyone else if you don't want to. The important thing is to know for yourself. A lot of folks go through life not knowing who they are or what they really want for themselves.

Women are particularly susceptible to the conditioning of leaving attention to themselves for last. This inevitably turns into us running out of time as we try to juggle the multiple responsibilities we have. The myriad of roles we take on somehow manage to become the totality of who we are without conscious thought as to our willingness to perform those roles. This doesn't mean you shouldn't perform the roles. The point is to recognize they are simply roles and that you get to CHOOSE how you participate in them.

At the same time, you must recognize that if you continue to focus your energy and efforts on everyone else and exclude yourself, you will more times than not burn out. This burn out can take various forms, from depression and anxiety to ulcers and migraines.

Those are examples of some extreme outcomes, but they are a reality for many women today.

Thankfully, there are ways to prevent them from developing and in cases where they have taken shape, you can take advantages of strategies and resources available to manage them. Some examples to consider are:

- Women's support groups (like Coffee & Conversation)
- Joining a gym for exercise
- Take classes
- Find a local walking/running group
- Block time for you in your schedule
- Therapy
- Unplug from technology for a set time
- Reading
- Listen to music
- Watch movies/TV
- Craft

This list isn't by any means all inclusive, but you get the idea. Make time for you. Ask yourself, "what have you done for me lately?"

Invest as much in you as you do for those you care about. You are worth it!

"Love yourself enough to set boundaries. Your time and energy are precious. You get to choose how you use it. You teach people how to treat you by deciding what you will and won't accept."

~Anna Taylor

BUT FIRST
COFFEE

Finding Self-Love & Self-Care

Michelle Keeler

As I reflect back on my life, I wonder how different my life could have been had I created the habit of asking myself about self-love or self-care and whether or not a change was needed. Asking one-self about your feelings and habits are not a part of the traditional mindset. I did not know self-care existed. I believe our mindsets are shaped by our environments, family, faith, religion and other influences. I believe my traditional mindset is part of the reason for me not loving myself fully and not understanding the importance of self-care.

I am a baby boomer, a spiritual individual with morals, values and integrity, a Libra who was born and raised in the Midwest with two parents and three brothers. I was raised in the era of tremendous upheaval and uncertainty in the midst of the Civil Rights Protest and the Black Power Movement; when racial discrimination and socioeconomic disparity were the norm. I was labeled because of my race, and also my gender. During this time my choices were limited with regard to where I could live, attend school, and shop. My career choices and employment opportunities were limited as well.

During my middle school years, my expression of self-love was believing I was a Black Panther. With a militant ideology I became actively involved in the movement. During my middle school years, I was part of the integration system and was bussed to a white school on the other side of town. For the majority of my school years I was often the only black in my class. The majority of the white teachers made me feel inadequate and unwanted leading to a lack of self-love and poor self-care.

As I grew into adulthood, I soon discovered that men ruled the world. A woman's place was generally seen as being in the home. Self-care and self-love was obtained by taking care of others. As I look back over my life, I realized that I was blessed to have a village of strong nurturing women who, in my eyes, were true feminists with a touch of class and sass. These women attempted to progress from being second- class citizens to create an environment of self-care and self-love.

I am a single mother of a beautiful Leo daughter who is my heartbeat. She is articulate, intelligent, an entrepreneur and is a nurturer as well. Her chosen profession is that of a Behavior Intervention Specialist who works with individuals with disabilities, and on the autism spectrum. It is funny how the fruit doesn't fall far from the tree. After having a discussion, I realize that she did not witness me or other women in her life engaging in self-care or expressing self-love. We now encourage and remind each other to engage in self-care and self-love on a daily basis.

I came into this world with the instinct to support and nurture people, a natural born caretaker, empathic and sensitive. I am there for every one and am able to give in a healthy nurturing way except to myself. I believe my passion in life is to let my light shine in this world of hurt. My profession of choice was to become a registered nurse. During my career I worked in various specialties, medical-surgical, obstetrics, gynecology, labor and delivery, pediatrics, chemical dependency as well as mental health and psychiatric nursing. I retired from the Department of State Mental Hospital. At this psychiatric facility I worked with the mentally incompetent and forensic individuals deemed criminally insane and committed through the criminal justice system.

I began to lose my objectivity and questioned my beliefs, and purpose as a result of working in unsupportive environments, being under-appreciated by people, and providing care to family members. I surrendered to the negativity and nastiness of the world. After being injured and taking retirement, I began to feel powerless, unloved, and unfocused.

I cried many tears, yelled at the universe and my higher power, began to live a life of a recluse. My self-worth got lost in translation for others to define and distort me. I gave control to their warped mindset of negativity, allowing ownership of my thoughts, feelings, actions and emotions.

I was living a life lost in grief, desperation, depression, disbelief, and self-pity. My SELF-CARE mindset was that of Self=**S-Silently-Evading- Life- Fearfully** while Care=**Carefully -**

Avoiding - Responsibility - Eroding away. Living and allowing FEAR=-**F-foolishly E-engaging - A-anger and R-rage** to overtake me. My physical look and posture became that of an aging person.

While on the path of brokenness, frustration, being lost and drowning in my own self- doubt and lack of worth, I forgot about forgiveness. I did not want to nor did I feel like forgiving. The truth is I really didn't know how or even had the desire to forgive. I knew I had to forgive myself first before others. I could not decide if forgiveness was a just a feeling or a decision. Even studying the word, devotions, prayer, meditation, reading self-help and psychology books, reaching out to spiritual leaders, family and friends and other holistic therapy did not help sway my mindset.

I now realize that self-care is me listening to my inner voice and forgiving myself and others in order to rebuild my self-respect, integrity, and trust despite knowing I will always remember the hurtful act. Forgiveness will ease the pain of consequences and memories so that I can move toward reconciliation with myself and those who I feel hurt me.

While at the lowest point in my season of loss, through grace my higher power and the universe ordered my steps toward some incredible individuals. I was led to follow a different path of self-discovery and self-care. This became my lesson in the best form of alleviating fear and reacquainting myself to self-love and self-care.

My self-care regime was to volunteer in the community, become more physically active by joining the GirlTrek movement of radical self-care and healing by daily walking and exercising. I became involved with the Yisrael Urban Family Farm helping to build community gardens and promoting their motto of "Transforming the Hood for Good."

I have also attended a variety of conferences and workshops. I participated in the AARP Back to Work 50+ program and a Career Path Development program of self-discovery to find my passions, transform my knowledge and skills to prepare me to transition into my next career.

During my journey on the road to self-discovery and self-care I learned to make the request out loud to God, my higher power, the universe, and my guardian angels.

Consequently, I am blessed to have found my tribe of beautiful, spiritual, intelligent African American women who are my bridge over troubled waters. They effortlessly and consistently uplift, support, encourage, and allow me to make mistakes without ridicule. They remind me daily of my greatness and gifts. I am beginning to see the African Queen and Braveheart in the mirror who is gaining clarity of her purpose, renewed faith, love and self- worth. I value and love myself. I once again feel confident in speaking my truth, remain virtuous, make decisions, and state NO as a complete answer without guilt.

I am learning to use emotional intelligence, personality assessments, the art of communication and conversation, along with I AM statements to state my passions, and career goals to move toward earning income for being the subject matter expert of myself (the SME of ME). I am forging my own brand by combining my gifts, talents, and wisdom for service to others. Having visual goals of myself as a practitioner, mentor, editor, author, entrepreneur, traveler and all around Shero. I could not be prouder or happier to allow my higher power, the universe and angels to manifest into my life.

My mindset today has gone from pessimism to optimism. These are my thoughts regarding what self-care really means.
SELF CARE = S-seeking to **E-evolve** in **L-love** and **life F-forever** while

C-consistently being **- Anchored** and **R-rising** in **E-excellence**

FEAR = F-forever – E-evolving A- amongst the **R-resistance….**

My affirmation:

I Am Light

I am able to take action in service to myself and others.

The fires of my authentic self-burn away any part that is unreal.

I easily move beyond limitations with
confidence and courage.
Humor invigorates my reality and I am
powerful…
I AM LIGHT.

Becoming A Better Me

Louise Umeki

I'm always striving to be extraordinary. I believe it's a journey that I am on.

Many years ago, as a single Mom, I worked my way up in business with little support from family and friends. When you're constantly working, constantly putting your child first, constantly doing for others, taking care of yourself takes a back seat. Your confidence gets lower and lower and lower because you are just surviving.

Recently, I was reminded of a past interview and remembered how important making small changes had impacted my life. Back then, just by doing something different for myself…something simple like putting on a little make-up, changing the way I styled my hair, or adding a new blouse and some sparkly jewelry, it would raise my confidence. In turn, people saw a change in me and that made me feel better.

It didn't take long for that to take effect. I set new dreams, goals, and visions to replace the old ones that were no longer serving me. I stopped listening to others who were telling me that what I wanted, either couldn't or wouldn't happen. I needed to believe in my goals so much so that I could taste, hear, feel, smell, and see them happening whether anyone else could or not. I trusted my own proven strategies. Once again, I know that I walk in faith, believe in miracles, and know that all things are possible with God. I know that I am a child of God blessed with a caring heart for those who are hurting, including me.

By setting new goals, I've realized the importance of how self-care shows up in my life and I've achieved positive results. I have lost weight and taken more time to journal and get back to my daily devotions. I've found and set boundaries, both in my personal and work lives. I rest and sleep more and enjoy the people who I've chosen to be in my daily life. Practicing self-care makes me feel like I'm worthy, not selfish. These new healthier habits remind me that I'm someone who deserves to have the best life I can.

Everyone who knows me knows that I love having fun. I love making emotional connections and have been very successful at building meaningful relationships. My son holds the biggest chunk of my heart without a doubt. However, my daughter-in-law and two awesome grandsons wouldn't have to battle at all for equal shares when it comes to lighting up my heart. As mom and grandma, I love them unconditionally and would do anything for them. They are truly the joys of my life. I love to cook and spend time with them and have been a dedicated soccer mom and grandma for over 35 years!

My fabulous four, like many friends who care, as well as those who rely on me, remind me that self-care is important…that self-care means purposefully taking care of myself. Sadly, I had a hard time trusting anyone but my son and his wife. I let people use me or walk all over me instead of saying no. I always wanted to help people even if it wasn't in the best interest for me.

Today, this is changing.

As I make more healthier choices and enjoy the benefits of self-care, I am tightening my sphere of influence, expanding my network, and enjoying being extraordinary. I am the Founder of PlannerCon, which is an annual International Conference for planning communities of all kinds. I also facilitate several smaller PlannerCon Party events throughout the year where vendors and attendees spend a long weekend sharing ideas and merchandise, creating presentations and workshops, and supporting a chosen non-profit all year long.

"Talk to yourself like you would to someone you love."

~Brene Brown

It's About Time

Deanna Vestal

Five years ago, I had no idea I was lacking confidence. I spoke to large and small groups on topics ranging from workforce preparation to HIV transmission and prevention. I never knew I felt unworthy of my dreams. I drove the car I wanted, and lived in my favorite neighborhood. It hadn't crossed my mind to ask if I felt lovable or not. When chaos whirled around me I felt like a victim of circumstance. There was always someone to blame for any misstep I took.

Funny how the veil of ignorance clouded my understanding. I was using my to-do lists, family, and community roles as coping mechanisms and I had no idea that I was walking a very high tight rope. When panic started to clench my chest and my fingers started going numb, I knew it was anxiety. I told myself it was stress, but I feared it was something life-threatening. When I found out I was physically healthy, I decided to take charge of my mental health. Looking back, it's so funny! I just knew that if I had better control of the people around me, I'd have less stress.

When I started my journey to manage others better, I did not associate it with self-discovery. I could rant off a situation that affected me or a past event that was obviously dramatic, but I could not tell you how it made me feel. I remember sharing an experience with my sister, Carolynn, and every time she asked how I felt about it, I went deeper into the story adding more particulars trying to explain how wrong the other person was. She was so persistent that I was compelled to pull up Google and type: "list of feelings." We laughed so hard my sides hurt. I was very out of touch with my own feelings. Even with a list I could only pinpoint judgement. I was not ready to admit that I was hurt, felt under-valued and disrespected.

The deep-dive to identify what I feel led me to an understanding that all relationships start with me. It was a very harsh eye-opener because on one hand, I am confident in who I am: smart, strong, successful, God-fearing, family-oriented. But I was learning that these are attributes awarded by what I do and who I associate with. Who I am is inside of me. My psyche, my thoughts, and my ego were completely incoherent. I called myself all kinds of names and lost confidence in my leadership style because I realized I did not know me. The chatter about me in my thoughts was harsher than I would ever allow someone to speak about one of my loved ones. That's how I realized I was the one who I needed in my corner. I am grateful for my studies which include, but are not limited to the 5 Love Languages, neurolinguistic programming, prayer, forgiveness, binaural beats, isochronic tones, fasting, and hot yoga.

Fast forward five years and self-care is an all-day every day practice. Sometimes I am in awe that I can observe my feelings and control my thoughts. I have developed the authority to relax my state of mind. I can imagine my scalp relaxed. My eyelids and my face. My throat, my neck, my shoulders, my hands, my abdomen, my thighs, my knees, my calves, my feet and my toes. Once upon a time I could not do that. When I draw attention to my consciousness I can focus on the expansion of my entire body. I close my eyes and envision a white light surrounding my entire body in a bubble. Peace, joy, and love resonates from me and I feel connected to Source energy, my Almighty God. I feel the light of Love surround me. I see myself for what I am: a piece of consciousness connected to the people I engage with every day.

I am eternally grateful for the mindset shift that occurs when I engage in proper breathing. I am so thankful for the wise old Sufisms, Dr. Joe Dispenza, Dr. Bruce Lipton, and Dr. Brene Brown who I found while researching ways to be. The new friendship with myself is wonderful. I am grateful for accepting myself as a woman who is whole, perfect and complete just as I am. I imagine myself giving me a hug and walking together with my ego thanking my ego for keeping me alert and allowing myself to be at peace lowering my defenses and envisioning beautiful moments in life. I am grateful for the abundance of feelings I now have full access to.

I release negative charges, anger, frustration, fear, and guilt that come up around people in my family who have wronged me, co-workers who misjudged me, friends who were enemies. I accept our connection and I imagine forgiveness as I ask them to forgive me. I speak to my negative emotions and repeat, "forgiveness is easy." I allow myself to rehash certain scenarios and I visualize aspects of forgiveness by observing why I feel how I feel.

My future is filled with joy, achievement, accomplishments and success. I work remotely and I travel with groups of people for work. We speak, learn, engage, and host trainings that include meditation, brain science, acts of service, and thought leadership; we contribute to the world. I have a personal trainer who helps me stay in shape; a personal chef who keeps me eating healthy foods, and I have a beautiful aura of acceptance and flow. My man and I are in love and we work well together. We dance, pray, eat, love, laugh, and motivate each other. We both enjoy good times, love youth, tell stories, and sing. Almighty God, let this or something better unfold in my life.

May all the beautiful things I've daydreamed unfold. Today, I ask for a perfect day filled with financial abundance, genuine connection, learning, creating, resting well, contributing to others in ways that manifest gratitude and mutual benefit. I see the truth in building a well aligned team of people who are change makers. I smell fresh fruits and vegetables. I am excited about our work together and the way we engage with each other and others. I am ready to be productive and rest well.

Almighty God, Ancestors, Spirit Guides, I feel the force of life that unites the entire world. I am honored with our connection. Please send blessings, energy, support and help me and every person reading this craft the perfect day that allows our dreams to unfold. I am happy and I enjoy being supported. I feel profound support from the scalp of my head and down my spine into my torso, my chest and legs. I feel energy embracing me and I know the universe has my back.

"Caring for your body, mind, and spirit is your greatest and grandest responsibility. It's about listening to the needs of your soul and then honoring them."

~Kristi Ling

Mindfulness as A Self-Care Practice

Robin Robinson-Myhand

At one of our coffee and conversation meeting we had a visitor who handed out flyers regarding mindfulness. The meetings are called "Melanin meets Mindfulness". The specific topic that was coming up was about Black Women and anger. I remember saying out loud this is what I need. I reviewed the articles that she provided and the flyers regarding monthly meetings. Later in the week I signed up for my first mindfulness meeting.

When I went to the meeting, I entered a room that was lush with comfy soft blankets on the floor, textured pillows, low lighting and candles. You could sit in chairs or relax on the floor with pillows. The colors were pastel and tranquil. I felt engulfed in luxury and found myself feeling peaceful and relaxed.

So, what is mindfulness?

Mindfulness means maintain a moment-by-moment awareness of our thoughts, feelings, bodily sensations, and surrounding environment, through a gentle and nurturing lens.

Simply put it is paying attention

- On purpose
- In the present moment
- Non judgmentally
- With compassion

In our meeting we discussed acceptance over resistance. When you are in an acceptance frame of mind you are open and when you are in a resistance frame of mind you are closed. Not much can happen when you are closed off. Being open minded and aware is where change and transformation can begin.

I learned how to find something neutral or pleasant to focus on when I'm angry or stressed. It's about self-soothing. Each of us had to figure out what we could do when we find ourselves in these situations. What works for me is focusing on my breathing and gently rubbing the top of my thighs just above my knees with my fingers. When I'm in a meeting this works. My hands are where no one can see them or at least one of them and I ground myself with breathing and bring awareness to the movement and feeling. It calms me down.

When I'm not in a meeting then I tend to get out and walk, sit outside and focus on what beauty is around me whether it be the trees, clouds, plants and breath or listen to guided meditations. There are so many apps that have 5, 10, 15, and 20-minute guided meditations. There are meditations for so many topics so part of the process is finding what resonates with you and whose voice resonates with you. The following are a few suggestions that I have on my phone:

- Liberate
- Mindfulness Coach
- Simple Habit
- Insight Timer

There are so many more. You can download them on your phone or tablet.

We also learned several acronyms that can help when things get rough, they are:

EASY and ICAN

They stand for:

Embrace **I**ntentionally

Accept — **C**entering

Surrender — **A**ttention

Yield — **N**ow

I find myself writing EASY a lot on my meeting notes and saying ICAN to myself.

We have discussed and will discuss other subjects at each meeting. Sometimes we have to revisit topics to further explore.

Mindfulness is a series of self-care techniques that can help us better manage our thought processes. These techniques enable us to take care of ourselves in the midst of our everyday busyness. In talking to people there is a misconception about mindfulness. It's not about stopping our thoughts and entering a state of thoughtless calm. Our minds tend to wander, it's simply how our minds work. When this happens, the way you can come back is to notice your breathing again. It's the act of bringing your attention back to a point of focus that is the essence of mindfulness.

Mindfulness is such a broad topic and you see it everywhere. There are products, books, magazines, coloring books, meditation apps, downloads and cd's, and certifications in mindfulness and they are all tied into self-care.

Another way I calm myself down and focus is to color. I have coloring books but have taken a huge liking to coloring on my phone. There are numerous apps for this. I tend to prefer the apps that are color by number. I like it because I don't have to make a decision about what color to color any area of the picture. I'm in the moment, following along and seeing how this picture with numbers that correspond to a color comes to life. For that time period I am focused just on that and nothing else and in the end, I have a beautiful colorful picture. I post them on Face Book or Instagram from time to time, so I get to share.

While in a book store I came across a magazine titled "Mindfulness" there. I noticed several magazines and books that talk about mindfulness and how to practice it. I purchased it and have now become a subscriber. The articles are very informative and uplifting. While there I saw numerous books on Mindfulness – it's very much the in topic for now.

While doing some reading, I came across another acronym COAL. I really like it and I want to leave you with this to keep in mind.

Curiosity – becoming mindfully aware is about discovery, so allow yourself to be surprised

Openness – don't get stuck by thinking there is only one approach to mindfulness

Acceptance – give both yourself and those around you a break

Love – love can be an everyday emotion where we show real kindness to ourselves and others

"It's not selfish to love yourself, take care of yourself, and to make your happiness a priority. It's necessary."

~Mandy Hale

Do You First

Linette Gill

Women are so powerful. We each have natural abilities and gifts that nurture our families, friends and sometimes even strangers. Our motherly instincts know when there is a problem and without hesitation, we immediately take action.

When we are fortunate enough to have women in our lives that are willing to share their experiences, creativity and strengths it is empowering and a blessing. Genuine concern for one another activates the law of reciprocity as we impart information, uplift and support one another.

Having productive interactions with others as we go about our day really depends on how well we have cared for ourselves. How can we be giving and understanding for others when we are in distress or have a need that is unmet? Yes, I know we support others regardless, but just imagine fulfilling your daily responsibilities, listening, counseling, giving support to others and it is not at your expense.

Our capacity to endure through unexpected challenges and achieve our own personal goals, is determined by the level of care we take for ourselves.

Oh, I know you care for yourself but, is it the first priority? I am guilty of this myself. I am disciplined in caring for everyone else first. I always tell myself, "I will do me later", but never get to me.

Whatever your "I will do me later" is, don't wait. Be your first priority. It is the most empowering action of your day.

Caring for yourself first creates opportunity to function in your fullest potential for yourself as well as for others. This is not a selfish daily mantra, but an act of preparation and thoughtfulness for all that you may encounter on your journey of life experiences.

All of us have family and work that come with responsibilities that dictate our time and emotions. While managing our life and navigating through it all, we will learn many things about ourselves and what we need along the way to be happy and whole. Most importantly, we will identify unique ingredients about ourselves; who we are, what we want and how we are going to achieve it.

Routines from my childhood greatly influenced how I cared for myself and I am sure that is true for most of us. Coming to the realization that how we think, act and believe is never concrete, is due to how our growth naturally reveals the need for us to make adjustments. It is not a bad thing or a rejection of the ones that nurtured you. Rather, it is positive progression on the strengths of the foundation that you have been given.

I have examined my life video tape in my mind, and have reflected on the ups and downs. The X Factor to staying on the up side, is caring for me first. I have learned who I am, what I want and how I am going to achieve it. I have learned to make adjustments along the way.

For me, being connected spiritually has always been a daily self-care ingredient. I was raised in a bible-based environment. Our family never missed going to church and bible study. My grandmother was a minister, so church was basically every day. It was all I knew. As a young adult I continued this religious routine. Church had been a place of refuge for my mind, soul and spirit my whole life.

As my life changed with marriage, three children and my two oldest children being disabled, I was unable to attend services regularly. I couldn't participate with the usual traditions and protocols of a religious lifestyle as I knew it. I felt confused and isolated. I was having a growth spurt and was forced to deal with a major shift in my religious foundation. I had to do things another way that would leave me feeling as if I was still whole spiritually. I had to make adjustments in my thought process on how I could still be connected to GOD. So, I created my own routine of prayer time and meditation. I found my own unique ingredients. My own spiritual place of peace.

Doing things your own unique way provides a visual form of communication to others concerning what works best for you. Be prepared for your personal preferences to be questioned or sometimes challenged. Especially when it is a family tradition. Stay confident and committed to your adjustments. This is called growing pains.

Growing pains are going to happen whether you are ready or not. Being determined to do things our own way may seem like an act of rebellion, but is only a necessary merging from one space of understanding and existence to another space of further potential. Our first reference of this merging of understanding within our existence is when we are 2. We are told about our tantrums and that we were terrible. But was it really terrible?

I would rename it exhausting rather than terrible. The patience required to help toddlers develop and navigate what they are feeling is simply exhausting. Well, guess what, it doesn't end there. We become adults still fighting for our unique thought process. Eventually we figure out our personal formula that makes us happy and learn to communicate effectively. Only you will know the essential ingredients. What is too much, what is too little or maybe not enough. It's your life and you get to do it your way. Exhausting no one else but yourself without the tantrums. Just care for yourself first so you will have the capacity when it is required of you to be patient or give to others.

One of my essential ingredients is prayer. First thing in the morning I need to pray over myself and then my family.

Speaking over my day with positive thoughts. Preparing for the known challenges and for the unexpected difficulties. It is not an option for me.

I must fill up my spiritual fuel tank so that I can endure all situations throughout the day. Being at peace with my adjustments has been life changing as well as strengthened my faith.

When weather permits, I enjoy walking just as the sun is rising. To me it is the most refreshing and spiritually uplifting time. Stretching by the park fountain and meditating with only the sound of water in the background feels like a small space of heaven on earth. I always believed that GOD would meet me where ever I was and knowing this allowed me to be ready to take on the day.

Another essential self-care ingredient for me is hot yoga. This is my favorite form of exercise and meditation. When I step on my mat, it's my sacred space. The room is empowered through unified discipline and focus. An unspoken respect and support for all that are present in the room. A silent rhythm along with the breathing techniques clears my mind of all the unhealthy thoughts in my life. It's emotionally soothing and cleansing. For me, it's not about doing a pose, but a physical metaphor of life. Functioning in a space for understanding of your body and its full existence and potential. Calm, controlled movements with consistency develops the capacity to achieve more each session. This spiritual, mental and emotional alignment energizes me.

There are times when situations can exhaust my fuel tank midway through the day. Fortunately, technology has added convenience and more opportunities to create a space for meditation anytime of the day. I enjoy listening to self-help and motivational podcasts to refuel my energy. I also use the prayer and calming apps which are just amazing. Staying calm and creating a peaceful atmosphere is a necessary discipline in my life. I can only accomplish what needs to be done with an optimistic and peaceful spirit.

Having these convenient tools to refuel throughout the day is extremely helpful when dealing with the expansion of responsibilities, friends, and business partners. This definitely can be overwhelming. Everyone wants a genuine social connection with others, but remember it can't be at the expense of your essential ingredients. Your needs must be a priority. Care for you first.

Navigating through our old and new social connections can be a challenging task. Unfortunately, you can't force a square peg into a round whole. Some people are only in your life for a specific reason and a season, while others may actually become close like a sibling for a lifetime.

There is an old cliché that says "the more the merrier." Would that work for you? How about "quality over quantity?" Some like crowds, but others prefer to be alone. Whichever social sphere you prefer, if you like it, then I love it. These are your essential ingredients. The point is to create your own standards and pick the space you desire to dwell in. There is nothing wrong with being aware of what is best for you.

Some of us have a full community to lean on while others may only have one sibling or a friend. Some may have no one at all. I purposely take the time to process these scenarios in my mind when I am having a rough day or week for that matter, because it keeps me grateful for the support and friends that I have.

My life experiences have revealed the essential ingredients that uniquely help me to be my best, while I continue to make adjustments as needed. Being available at full capacity daily is always my goal. I have labeled myself as an "extra credit" individual. All that know me will probably agree.

So, by staying committed to my self-care routine and thought process of being me, my way, I have a continuously growing social group of likeminded individuals that are extra credit too. Now that's funny! We have a wonderful time being extra credit together.

Your life experiences have shown you who you are, what you want and how you are going to achieve it. You are a powerful being that provides support and inspiration. Tap into your nurturing power that you give everyone else and do it for you. Stand firm in your convictions. Embrace your authentic self, loyal to your passions and committed to your goals. Fully embrace your authentic self and independence of thought. Be available. Allowing the law of attraction to seek out and reveal those that compliment your unique ingredients that are essential in your life.

Keep caring for you first.

Now go be your best, by doing you, your way.

Coffee and Conversation

Phillis Clements

It's only fitting that there be something in the book that talks about what our community is all about. While this is the fourth volume of the book, it is the sixth year of existence for the group Coffee and Conversation. I can hardly believe it.

I can still remember the day in March of 2013 when I sat at a table in a room of more than 300 people and spoke with a woman I didn't know, who had the most wonderful energy about her. I remember thinking, "well here's your chance to see if what you're thinking is a crazy idea or a concept that women would be willing to be a part of." So, I asked if she would be interested in participating and she said, "yes." We have since become like sisters.

I've always known that I would find a way to bring people together to share our gifts, wisdom and love. It has been such a blessing to have met so many wonderful women and developed friendships that are truly heartfelt.

The Coffee & Conversation community was created to provide an environment for women to experience positive encouragement, a sense of empowerment, inspiration, and support. Every month the group brings together powerful, wise and liked-minded women who want to provide a way to promote a progressive mindset in the world around us. A progressive mindset is one that focuses on positive growth versus one that is set on tradition and generally opposed to change. We believe in building positive and supportive relationships.

Positive relationships are critical to the success of any community. In order to develop positive relationships, we have to begin with the basics – civility, courtesy, consideration, and kindness. In order to ensure that the basics are met, we must become good communicators. Communication is an exchange between two or more parties. To be an effective communicator one should understand the most important factor is the ability to listen. Listening to understand, not to be understood.

The need to unlearn the bad habit of thinking about our response before the person has even finished saying what they have to say can be a challenge. This is an especially difficult habit to break because it is part of our social norms. While learning to anticipate the needs of others is an attribute that is very useful, we have to also learn when it is appropriate to act on what we believe may be needed. You will not find in the definition of communication a description that says no one should be listening, only speaking.

Here are some tips to follow for effective communication.

- Be present.
- You must focus on what is being said.
- Look at the person speaking.
- Ask for clarification about those thoughts expressed that are unclear. Doing this will demonstrate your intent to understand; and more times than not, you will benefit from this effort greatly.

You can't expect to receive what you aren't willing to give. What better way to practice effective communication skills is there than to do so over coffee? Fun fact - - coffee is the second most consumed beverage on the planet.

During our meetings we practice the art of listening and learn something new each and every time. Our sessions are always insightful, inspiring, full of laughter, and just plain fun. As women, we have a lot on our plates and we need to be around others who understand what we go through, to hold us up when we are falling down, and to praise us when we are being magnificent.

Coffee and Conversation gives us this and more. Through our community bond we have built more self-confidence, increased our self-esteem, and developed trust. New businesses have been launched, careers are thriving and new friendships have blossomed.

There are not enough words to describe how wonderful it is to be a part of such an amazing group of women who are truly invested in being the best we can be and accept each other as we are. There is no judgement. This is a safe and sacred space.

It is very empowering to know and feel the genuine desire for friendship, sisterhood and a community bond that facilitates personal growth of the mind, body and spirit.

THANK YOU, ladies of Coffee & Conversation!

"Women have to take the time to focus on our mental health—take time for self, for the spiritual, without feeling guilty or selfish. The world will see you the way you see you, and treat you the way you treat yourself."

~Beyoncé

Author Biographies

Kenya Aissa

KENYA E. AISSA, MS has over 30 years of experience as a teacher, youth advocate, public speaker, and social worker, specializing in adolescent and teen girls with trauma. Kenya lives with her husband and son in the San Francisco Bay Area.

Kenya is an accomplished actress, makeup artist and yoga instructor. She recently released her first book *Sacred Girl: Spiritual Life Skills for Conscious Young Women,* which can be purchased online from Amazon.

Kenya may be reached at rubyenvy@gmail.com.

Jean J. DiGiacomo

Jean is a woman doing her best to meet life on life's terms. She is 60 years old, a newly retired teacher, the widow of a kind and loving man, the mother of a fabulous 22-year-old son, in a committed relationship with an amazing partner and has been sober for 2,492 days. Jean has never liked Pina Coladas (not even as an active drunk) and loathes getting caught in the rain. While she loves the feel of the ocean, Jean thinks making love at midnight in the dunes of the cape may sound terribly romantic in theory but is likely to result in sand in complicated places. Jean is contemplating yoga, and wishes she loved health food, but doesn't.

Thankfully, she has half a brain. Jean is gratefully living her perfectly imperfect life. She is humbled to be included in this compilation of writings by such extraordinary women.

Instagram: @jj_planswithlove
Email: jjDiGiacomo@comcast.net

Linette Gill

Linette Gill is a realtor, mentor to families of disabled loved ones and wife of 30 years. She is a mother of 2 sons and a daughter. Over the past 27 years she has developed skills to help her disabled sons and others alike. She quickly became known as the "special needs" counselor in her constantly growing social sphere. In addition, she is licensed and certified to own and operate 24/7 care facilities for veterans, elderly and the disabled.

As one of the founding families of the UC Davis M.I.N.D. Institute and a current board member, Linette's philanthropic efforts reflect her commitment to science and research of neuro-development. She is now developing a Diverse and Alternative Parenting Consultant business. The service will be one of many offered under her non-profit organization Amara Helps, which is scheduled to launch January 2020.

She can be reached at linettegillrealtor@gmail.com

Pauline Haynes

Pauline Haynes is a Life Coach with the uncanny ability to help you identify what truly inspires you and helps you focus your life around those things that bring you joy, peace and satisfaction. She also delights in the officiating of sacred marriage ceremonies

The wide range of life experiences Pauline brings to the table includes parenting two children, who are in turn living their purpose-filled, successful and happy lives! She has navigated the daily challenges and opportunities of living in three different countries, and among diverse cultures. In addition to many volunteer hours of working with people living with AIDS, Crisis intervention, Emotional Emancipation Facilitation, serving on the board of arts communities, and other heart related endeavors, her varied career has taken her from being a massage therapist, a Hospice care worker, a radio talk show host, a personal chef, an event planner, a leader of women's workshops and retreats, a cultural awareness trainer/facilitator, an art curator and promoter, among other things. It is precisely because of Pauline's intuitive nature, and her "out of the damn box" way of thinking that gives her the edge when working with clients.

The words that sum up Pauline's philosophy of life is Shift Happens! Do or Do Not. There is no try.

Pauline is happy, fulfilled, pursuing her purpose and gets tremendous joy from her eight grandchildren and friends. She lives in Sacramento.

www.paulinehaynes.net

Jacquelyn S. Howard

Jacquelyn Smithson Howard is a freelance writer and poet, originally from Nashville Tennessee. Her love of poetry began shortly after her Aunt foretold of this poetic destiny, in the first grade.

Jacquelyn learned then, that the poems and short stories came without warning. She learned to listen and write them down, no matter the time or place. She also learned that the poems were meant to become part of the ethos. She writes from her own life experiences, and shares them at local poetry venues and in other social circles.

Jacquelyn is known as the Giggle and Smooch Storyteller, explaining that she had never heard her parents raise their voices in anger with each other. They communicated with love and respect for one another, and were the original members of the Giggle and Smooch Club. She hopes to create Giggle and Smooch Clubs wherever she speaks.

Jacquelyn is a member of the ZICA Literary Guild, and her poetry has been published in their 3rd Anthology and many other anthologies. She is a member of the Keynote Poets and Writers of Sacramento, and has been featured at several local creative arts venues. She is a regular at Sacramento's Open Mic scene.

Jacquelyn currently lives in Elk Grove, California.

She can be reached at
itsmytimetosoar@gmail.com.

Lauren Keeler

Lauren was born in Kansas and grew up in northern California as an only child of a single mother and has two dogs. She spends most of her free time with friends and family.

Lauren is a lover of music and all things creative. Throughout life she has enjoyed dance, art, and travel. She possesses a master of science degree in psychology (applied behavior analysis) and is currently working as a behavior intervention specialist for a school district. She is also embarking on becoming an entrepreneur.

Michelle Keeler

Michelle Keeler is a Kansas native. She is a mother to an exceptional daughter, registered nurse, natural nurturer, caregiver and empath. A woman who is a traditional, solid, productive and service oriented individual, that enjoys utilizing her skills and knowledge to promote love and healing to others.

After retiring from a career in Psychiatric, Behavioral and Mental Health nursing, she is currently on a self- paced journey of exploration into self-care, self-love, career- development, the art of communication through facilitated conversation, spiritual growth and self - discovery. She is manifesting that her higher power and the universe allows her to use her knowledge, faith, wisdom, passion and skills to earn a living for being paid for being herself. During her transition she is attending workshops and taking classes. Currently she has found a tribe of like-minded African- American female hybrid practitioners who are uplifting her to flourish in her journey.

She is beyond grateful to her God and Phillis Clements of Sunshine Solutions for this first-time opportunity of self-expression to be published.

Michelle may be reached at
md.keeler.mk@gmail.com.

Angela Lofton-Moore

Angela Lofton Moore started writing poems and stories in part to help her master the English language that she needed to learn in order to communicate with those around her. The daughter of an Air Force family, she was born and raised in Berlin, Germany and moved to Sacramento, California at age 11 unable to speak much more than just a few words of English. That hurdle forced her to become creative very quickly and writing became a valuable tool. That love for writing has never left her and she became a life-long lover of the written word.

Angela left the corporate world of voice and data network design and started InfoPrincess Graphics, in 2009. In 2016, she formed MoorePark Enterprises LLC, opened WorkFlow Lounge, a Coworking space where Coffee & Conversation meets, in 2017 and created a nonprofit organization, Beyond The Village, in 2018. Her life is hectic, but she wouldn't change it for the world. Her chapter in this book, Self-Discovery |

Self-Love | Self-Care | Self-Discipline, is her personal guide to how she handles the daily stress of running 3 companies and a nonprofit.

Angela still loves being able to utilize her creativity whenever possible to design for her clients. In her spare time, she continues to write erotic fiction, poetry and real-life stories, but until the first Coffee & Conversation book was released in 2016, her personal writings had never been published.

Angela is excited to, for the third time, have her work published alongside an amazing group of "Coffee & Conversation" women, and she continues to be thankful to have her wonderful husband of 27 years, Sidney, by her side supporting her in all of her creative endeavors.

To learn more about Angela, please visit her website or social media pages.
Website: www.angelaloftonmoore.com
Facebook.com/angelaloftonmoore
Twitter.com/angelalbmoore
Instagram.com/angelaloftonmoore
Email: angelaloftonmoore@outlook.com

Robin Robinson-Myhand

Robin Robinson-Myhand is a Personal Development Guide, author, speaker and owner of New Phase of Life. She provides guidance, resources and tools that encourage, empower and equip people to embrace their own unique greatness and find their own unique path.

Her professional and personal experiences have provided her with the skill set to help people to embrace self-confidence and to reach their full potential while being true to themselves.

She is a certified personal development coach and a certified mediator.

Robin can be reached at

Website: www.newphaseoflife.com
Email: robin@newphaseoflife.com
Facebook: Robin Robinson Myhand
Facebook Group: A Better Me (for women only)
Instagram: @robmrob

Joy Normand

Joy Normand is the founder of Equipping U 4 Excellence. Joy is driven by a desire to provide resources that equip and empower women. She is passionate about helping women fulfill their God-given purpose and destiny.

Joy is a gifted mentor, motivator and speaker. Joy has shared with thousands of listeners through speaking engagements and serving as a worship leader. However, one of the titles she holds dearest to her heart is that of being a wife, mother and nana! Equipping U 4 Excellence hosts women's events and provides resources that equip women to handle life's difficulties while enriching their hearts, encouraging their passions and expanding their professional and personal dreams.

Joy's goal is to help you achieve deep awareness about who you are, what you want, what gets in your way, and how to overcome it. To learn more about Joy's workshops and training, visit her website at www.equippingufully.com.

Jean E. Robinson

Jean Evans Robinson is a retired public-school teacher who lives in Sacramento, California with her two cats, Thelma and Louise.

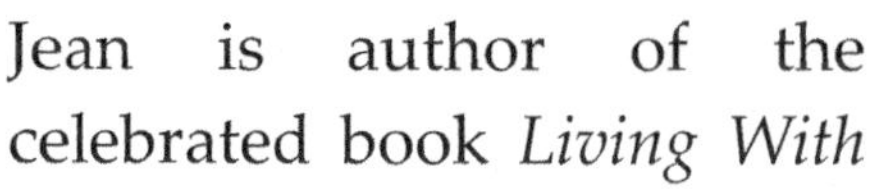

Jean is author of the celebrated book *Living With Duplicity,* published by Sunshine Solutions Publishing, and can be found on most online shopping sites. Her poetry can be found in "Dime Show Review" Volume 1, Issue 1 published by 88 Poets Press.

She is presently writing a sequel to her novel "Living With Duplicity" and is working on a play from her novella "The Switch: A Railroad Maid's Story".

She would like to thank her family and friends for their support and encouragement.

Louise Umeki

Louise Umeki is a woman of action and believes in bringing and connecting people together, inspiring everyone to just be who we are.

Louise is the founder and creator of PlannerCon, an international conference for planners held in the San Francisco Bay area of northern California. Along with this annual event that boasts over 1,000 attendees, she conducts smaller PlannerCon parties in various cities across the United States throughout the year. She is also the founder of the business training and networking expo Powerful Possibilities in Elk Grove, CA that meets monthly.

As a dynamic innovator of community building and personal development, Louise strives to encourage and empower others to believe that anything is possible.

You can reach Louise at

sparklewithlouise@yahoo.com

Deanna Vestal

Deanna graduated from the University of Phoenix where she currently holds positions as President - Sacramento Alumni Chapter UOPX and VP Alumni Leadership.

It is her pleasure to assist executives with clarifying business strategies in specific areas of workforce development.

She is passionate about spending time with individuals and groups, matching personalities for optimal team performance, and facilitating conversations among decisions makers.

Her focus is on building healthy relationships in the workplace, identifying personal values and generating career path clarity.

You can reach Deanna at

Email: Deanna.Vestal@cpdonline.net

www.linkedin.com/in/dvestal

About the Publisher

Phillis Clements is an ontologist, influencer, educator, sought-after speaker, and CEO. She has over 30 years of experience in the corporate world, was an adjunct professor for the Los Rios Community College District and is an independent book publisher with several books of her own in print. All of her books are available online via popular online retailers like Amazon.com and Barnes & Noble, as well as her website.

Her women's empowerment group Coffee & Conversation; for which this book is named, continues to grow as she promotes an environment of positivity, inspiration, action and encouragement. It is her dream to see the group go global by establishing chapters of likeminded women around the world.

For more information, contact her at reachme@phillisinspires.com, join the Coffee & Conversations group on Facebook or visit her website www.sunshinesolutions7.com.

Join us today!

References

friend. 2018. In Merriam-Webster.com. Retrieved May 8, 2018, from https://www.merriam-webster.com/dictionary/friend

friendship. 2018. In Merriam-Webster.com. Retrieved May 8, 2018, from https://www.merriam-webster.com/dictionary/friendship

Covey, Stephen R. (1989), *7 Habits of Highly Effective People*. New York, New York: Simon & Schuster

Unless otherwise indicated, all scripture quotations are taken from the *Holy Bible*, King James Version.

RAINN.org, UK Violence Intervention and Prevention Program. Retrieved May 16, 2015, from https://rainn.org/articles/self-care-after-trauma?_ga=2.151907321.1542102834.1572392612-540141750.1572392612

Famous Quotes at BrainyQuote. Retrieved from www.brainyquote.com.

Self-Care quotes at Habits for Well Being. Retrieved October 31, 2019 from https://www.habitsforwellbeing.com/20-quotes-to-inspire-self-care/

Self-Care quotes at Develop Good Habits. Retrieved November 1, 2019 from https://www.developgoodhabits.com/self-care-quotes/

www.thecancerjourney.com

www.thespiritofwater.com